Meet My Cats

MUPPET

GEMMA

GABRIELLE

CHESTERTON

TWIGLET

MALTEAZER

OCTOPUSSY

AGNEATHA

MOTLEY

SPIRO

AMON-RA

BLOSSOM

With love to Enid

PUFFIN PIED PIPER BOOKS
Published by the Penguin Group
Penguin Books USA Inc., 375 Hudson Street, New York, New York 10014, U.S.A.
Penguin Books Ltd, 27 Wrights Lane, London W8 5TZ, England
Penguin Books Australia Ltd, Ringwood, Victoria, Australia
Penguin Books Canada Ltd, 10 Alcorn Avenue, Toronto, Ontario, Canada M4V 3B2
Penguin Books (N.Z.) Ltd, 182-190 Wairau Road, Auckland 10, New Zealand
Penguin Books Ltd, Registered Offices: Harmondsworth, Middlesex, England

First published in hardcover in the United States 1989 by Dial Books
A Division of Penguin Books USA Inc.

Published in Great Britain by HarperCollins Publishers
Copyright © 1989 by Lesley Anne Ivory
All rights reserved
Library of Congress Catalog Card Number: 89-1526
Printed in Hong Kong
First Puffin Pied Piper Printing 1994
ISBN 0-14-054920-X
1 3 5 7 9 10 8 6 4 2

A Pied Piper Book is a registered trademark of
Dial Books
A Division of Penguin Books USA Inc.,
® TM 1,163,686 and ® TM 1,054,312.
MEET MY CATS
is also available in a hardcover
and a miniature hardcover edition from Dial Books.

Meet My Cats

LESLEY ANNE IVORY

A Puffin Pied Piper

Meet My Cats

I have always had cats about me and they have played a big part in my life. Now I have twelve, unplanned—but essential to me.

I was an only child and when I was five, kittens were born in the coal barn next door. Mother said I might have one, and I can still remember the day when Auntie Tot brought Tissy around to me. Tissy and I grew up together and he was there all through my school days. It was not until after I was married with a four-year-old son, James, that I had another cat.

Honey chose us. He insisted that we buy him when we went to the pet shop to get a kitten. Just before Julian, my second son, was born, I adopted Tickle, whose family was moving to America, and I also had Phuan, my first pedigree Seal Point Siamese. So by now, we had three.

Tissy   Tickle   Honey   Phuan

And when, one morning, I saw an irresistible brown tabby in the market, it seemed only natural to rescue him and so we brought him home. We called him Top Cat—TC for short.

Ruskin was rescued from an unhappy home by James. He is now a huge, magnificently rich Persian. At the same time that Ruskin joined our family I also acquired Mau-Mau, a Tabby Point Siamese. And then one day, coming home from school, the boys and I went the long way around, and I bought Gemma—my first girl, and the oldest of the twelve cats we have today.

TC   Ruskin and Mau-Mau   Gemma

Gemma

Gemma is a silver, spotted tabby with a white blouse and socks to match. She has a passion for feathers. I used to keep a bunch in my studio, but she removed them one by one and hid them behind a cushion in the sitting room.

I had heard that cats like to have their kittens alone, so when Gemma's kittens were ready to be born, I prepared her "nest" and left her in the kitchen. But she came and called me in from the garden, led me into the house, turning around all the time to make sure I was following. And there on the kitchen cart behind a Save the Children dish towel, she had four kittens—two boys and two girls.

We kept the two girls, Muppet and Emu, and found wonderful homes for the boys, Lou and Bimbo.

Muppet

Sadly, we lost Emu in a road accident, but Muppet grew into a striking coal-dark tabby, very soft and velvety. She has a white locket at her throat inherited from her mother's white blouse.

Muppet always tucks us in at night, first kneading me in for a good ten minutes, staring hard at me and purring her lullaby. She then moves over and repeats the whole thing with my husband before curling up between us.

Muppet is the most adept refrigerator opener. Once she managed to extract half a chicken so many times I had to give it to her—and buy a new fridge, which has an anti-Muppet device on it! When she was a year old, she gave birth to five kittens in our closet—all with the Muppet white locket. Of these five we kept one, Gabrielle.

MEDIA CENTER
RAYMOND MIDDLE SCHOOL

Gabrielle

Gabby, or the little black Gabardine as we sometimes call her, poses so elegantly for me to paint her. She is a real chatterbox and never stops chirruping all over the house. She will knock at the front door to be let in, and then slink onto your lap as soon as you have sat down.

She loves chasing and retrieving a ball of paper, which she then drops at your feet for another throw. Sometimes she returns it to a pair of shoes and then wonders why it is not thrown again.

Gabby is also very good at retrieving the neighbors' leftover food, which they put out for the birds. Once she was seen returning twelve times to collect twelve stale buns from the neighbors' lawn to our lawn.

Sadly she cannot stand her granny, Gemma, who hissed at her soon after she was born. Gabby has never forgiven her, and screams every time she meets her.

Twiglet

The coming of Twiglet was a bit different. We had originally bought him for the boys' granny, who wanted a little, well-behaved cat. We said we would buy her a nice tabby in the pet shop where Gemma came from.

On the way to Granny's, Julian and he became hopelessly attached to each other, and were very sad to part. So both Twiglet and Julian were overjoyed when Granny telephoned the next day to say that after one night of Twiglet she felt she could not cope with him at all! We absorbed him into our family with joy. He and Julian were inseparable and Twiglet would wait for his return from school every day.

He spends ages sitting on the kitchen drain board, watching the faucet drip and patting the drops as they fall. He also adores toast and marmalade, often sharing my husband's breakfast, and has found out how to get the best out of a full milk carton; the nearer the bottom he bites, the longer the jet of milk.

Chesterton and Malteazer

Twiglet and Gabby had three children, also born in our closet. We called them the Triplikits. Like their mother, they were inveterate talkers and conversations lasted all night. We kept two of them, Chesterton and Malteazer. All the Triplikits had the Muppet white locket, a family legacy.

Twiglet kept close tabs on his kittens and visited them regularly in the closet, helping to wash them at night. While they were actually being born he came to visit Gabby and saw black-and-white Chesterton coming into the world. The sight of it made him take to his heels and rush into the bathroom, where he all but fell out of the window! He just put on his brakes in time.

They are still a united family and Twiglet is very proud of them. He guarded and guided their childhood games, especially in the garden, and kept all dangers at bay. He even rescued them from trees when they got stuck.

Spiro and Blossom

Spiro was in the local pet shop and the boys said he was going to be alone all weekend. After lunch on Saturday we went to the shop and bought him. He was a soft, pale, honey-ginger.

He grew into a really big boy, and was the ringleader (with, I think, Chesterton and Twiglet) in some especially naughty adventures. Our neighbor two doors away sportingly said to me, "Your cats know when I've put bones in the garbage can, *one* can't lift the lid alone, but *three* can, and your ginger tom and two more circle the can, put shoulders to the lid, and on a cat-count of 'one, two, three, *off* with it boys,' off it comes and in they go!"

Only a few weeks after Spiro came, we were in town buying shoes for Julian. He and his father rather unwisely left me for a short time, and there in the pet shop was Blossom. I bought her at once as a present for Spiro, popped her on top of a bag of oranges, and waited for the others innocently.

Blossom grew up with Spiro and they had wonderful games together: chasing through the flowers and romping among clean, preferably freshly ironed clothes.

Agneatha

One year we went to Cornwall for a vacation and James stayed at home to look after the cats. We telephoned him every evening to see how everybody was and one evening, about halfway through the vacation, he said to his father, "Tell Mom all nine are doing well." But we only had eight, and no kittens were imminent. It meant only one thing. He had acquired another!

Agneatha, named after the blonde in Abba, James's favorite group, blew over the floor to meet us when we arrived home. She was totally captivating, a little fluffy tortoiseshell and white ball.

Agneatha was a perfect kitten. She stayed beside me and slept in her basket, followed me into the garden and played with little flower seed heads. Her fur grew fluffier and we realized we had a little Persian on our hands. She became one of the most popular cats on my designs and was a wonderful model.

Agneatha had two litters, a total of nine kittens—and she is now a grandmother to twenty-eight more by her daughter, Avril.

Agneatha's first litter

Agneatha chose April 1, the day before James's twenty-second birthday, to have her first litter of four kittens, born in a special box with a window cut in it. There was a spotted silver tabby, Manuel, two little tortoiseshells, Avril and April, and lastly a little ginger one that she was particularly fond of.

The kittens grew all too soon and the agonizing business of parting with them came around again. The ginger, Dillon the Second, now known as D2, only went across the road to friends, so it was not really like seeing him leave home.

Agneatha's second litter

When Agneatha's second litter arrived (only four months later), D2 came over regularly to play with them. There were five kittens this time, of which we kept two: a richly marked tabby, Octopussy, so called because he was the eighth kitten born on the eighth day of the eighth month, and little Motley, a dark tortoiseshell.

I made weight and progress charts of all the kittens born in our house. Every one was a good size, averaging five ounces at birth. A house with kittens in it has a special contented aura. My mother made them weird and wonderful cloth toys, with wool whiskers and sinister tails. They would go mad with these, frisking them in the air and biting them to pieces. Octopussy loved one in particular, stole it from his sister, Motley, and hid it under a pair of Julian's shoes.

Amon Ra (Ra-Ra)

Ra Ra was a complete surprise! One Easter, James planned a "different" Easter egg for me—in fact a *Siamese* chocolate point Easter egg. He was convinced I *needed* it. I must admit, the sight of this wondering, pale, ethereal little being with cornflower eyes staring anxiously out of his wrappings at me, did rather catch me a bit off guard.

Suddenly we had twelve. This was a case of one more really making a tremendous amount of difference. Ra Ra is extremely active and mischievous, and has a gift of turning on the amazed, innocent blue stare if one of my precious Greek plates mysteriously "falls" from the dresser or an egg drops from its basket if he only passes by. If he wants anything, he keeps asking for it in increasingly loud meows. He is loving and bites our chins and chews our hair; it is a very good thing for him that we love him too.

And now there are twelve

All the cats love it when we are in the garden with them, and they set up elaborate games to impress us. They dash through the flowers, spring out at us, slap our legs, and then rush madly up the trees, ears flat back for speed.

Twelve really is quite a crowd, but they are my inspiration and joy and the essence of my paintings and my life. I shall always have cats about me.

MUPPET

GEMMA

GABRIELLE

CHESTERTON

TWIGLET

MALTEAZER

OCTOPUSSY

AGNEATHA

MOTLEY

SPIRO

AMON-RA

BLOSSOM

About the Author

Well-known for her paintings on cards, calendars, and gifts, Ms. Ivory also illustrated *Cats Know Best* by Colin Eisler (Dial), praised by *School Library Journal* as "the essence of cats perfectly depicted." More recently Ms. Ivory wrote and illustrated *Cats in the Sun* about which *Kirkus Reviews* said, "Pictures of cats and kittens blissfully enjoying their several settings will delight cat-lovers of all ages." Ms. Ivory and her family live in Hertfordshire, England.